A *Guide to*
Fresh
Herbs

When to Snip
What to Crush
How to Enjoy

Printed in the United States of America
by G&R Publishing Co.

Published By:

CQ Products
507 Industrial Street
Waverly, IA 50677

ISBN-13: 978-1-56383-333-5
ISBN-10: 1-56383-333-6
Item #7096

Fresh herbs

With a return to the "simple" life for many, as well as the "sophistication" of our palates and dining experiences, gardeners and cooks alike are becoming more aware of the wonderful world of fresh herbs and the power they have in the kitchen. Incorporate the bold punch of fresh herbs into your cooking, whether homegrown or purchased, and you will be well on your way to becoming a true gourmet!

Herbs are sometimes defined as seed plants which do not develop persistent woody tissue and die down at the end of a growing season. Other times, herbs are narrowly defined by comparison to spices; herbs consist of fresh leaves and stems or crumbled or powdered dried leaves, while spices include seeds, stems, roots and berries which have been dried for use in whole, ground or powdered forms. Still others define herbs more broadly as plants whose leaves, stems, roots or flowers are used for food or medicine.

The fresh herbs in this guide have been selected for their familiarity, cuisine enhancement capabilities and ability to be grown by the home gardener.

Tips for gardening & harvesting

Growing
+ Planting your herbs in the southernmost sunny spot of the garden will help plants receive the most light.
+ A raised bed, 10 inches or more off the ground, provides better drainage.
+ When purchasing plants, be sure they are meant for culinary use. Ornamental varieties are bred for appearance rather than taste and may be inedible.
+ Water herbs in the morning. Since they generally prefer to be dry, this allows them time to dry through the day.

Container Gardening
+ Use only soil mixes formulated for containers.
+ Cover the holes in the bottom of the pots with a small piece of window screen or weed cloth. Gravel or pottery shards can interfere with drainage.
+ Choose containers large enough to support a mature root system and hold plenty of soil.
+ Fertilize frequently and evenly. Maintain an appropriate moisture level.

Harvesting
+ Herbs are ideally harvested on a dry day following two consecutively dry days. Cut the herbs in the morning, as

soon as the dew has evaporated and before the sun warms the leaves. Herbs' oils are strongest in the morning.

+ For the best growth, harvest herbs often and prior to flowers blossoming. If annual plants are allowed to flower and produce seeds, they will quit growing leaves.
+ Generally, a perennial herb can be cut back to about half its height and an annual herb down to a few inches.

Tips for storage & preservation

Fresh Herbs
+ To keep purchased herbs at their best, remove any rubber bands or fasteners and trim the root ends and lower stems.
+ Wait to wash fresh herbs until just before use, as excess moisture in the refrigerator will shorten their shelf life.

Dried Herbs
+ Wash herbs for drying with cool water immediately after gathering and gently pat them dry with a towel.
+ Some herbs can be dried as stripped leaves (basil, mint, and tarragon) and others can be dried on the stems and stripped after drying (oregano, savory, thyme and rosemary).
+ Hanging leaves downward will allow the essential oils to flow from stems to leaves. Hang in a dark, warm (70° to 90°F), well-ventilated, dust-free location.
+ To prevent dust from collecting on the drying herbs, tie a perforated, loose paper bag around them. (The bag must have plenty of holes in it to remain fully ventilated.)
+ Herbs can dry in 3 to 4 days or 1 to 2 weeks, dependending on conditions. The faster they dry, the more flavor they retain. If the weather has been humid, additional dry-time of a few minutes in an oven at 125°F may be helpful. Make sure herbs are completely dry before storage to prevent mold growth.
+ Dried whole leaves and seeds retain flavor better, so crush or grind herbs just before use rather than before storage.
+ Store dried herbs in airtight containers in a cool, dry, dark location. Discard herbs with a musty or "flat" aroma.
+ Basic guidelines for shelf-life of properly or commercially dried herbs:
    + Whole leaves – 2 years
    + Whole seeds – 2 to 3 years
    + Crushed or cut – 1 year
    + Ground – 6 months

Frozen Herbs
+ Experiment with freezing methods to find what is best

for your situation. Because frozen herbs become limp and tend to lose color, they are best used in cooked foods and not suitable for garnishing.

+ Herbs frozen with water in ice cube trays are best used in liquid dishes such as soups or stews.
+ Use freezer bags, rather than plain plastic bags, for the best results when storing herbs in the freezer.
+ Store frozen herbs for 2 to 6 months.

Always label containers of preserved herbs with the herb's name and the date.

Tips for the kitchen

+ For most recipes, unless otherwise directed, mince fresh herbs into tiny pieces. Use a very sharp knife or kitchen shears when preparing herbs. Fine chopping will release more oils and flavor into your food. Grinding or crushing herbs will also produce flavorful results by releasing oils.
+ Rinse fresh herbs gently with cool water just before use. Prepare herbs close to the time of use to maintain the most flavor and the least wilting.
+ To chop large leaves "chiffonade-style" (thin strips), simply stack a few leaves, roll them up and use a sharp knife to cut the strips.
+ In general, ¼ teaspoon ground herb = 1 teaspoon dried herb = 1 tablespoon fresh herb. More success is found substituting fresh herbs for dried, rather than the other way around.

Tips on safety

+ Always grow and cook with varieties of herbs intended for culinary use; do not eat herbs or flowers from florists as they have often been treated with pesticides or preservatives not intended for consumption.
+ Never consume plants whose identity is uncertain; although the common name may sound like an edible plant, it may not be, and could even be poisonous.
+ The processes and lengths of time for storage are merely suggestions. Use common sense and individual evaluation to determine the quality and safety of anything consumed.

Fresh Herbs A-Z 6-59

Classic Herb Combinations 60

Terms 60

Anise

What is it?

Anise is a dainty annual herb which grows to about 2 feet in height, with finely cut, serrated leaves and flat clusters of small white or yellow flowers. The dry fruit of anise splits open when mature to reveal the tear-shaped seed. Aniseed, the most widely known portion of the plant, is used whole or crushed in curry powders, cakes, pastries, candies, cheeses and sauces. Anise oil is used for flavoring many beverages while the leaves can be enjoyed as a garnish or as an addition to salads. This relative of parsley is native to the Eastern Mediterranean region.

Flavor profile

Anise is aromatic with a sweet taste and licorice flavor.

Growing & harvesting tips

+ Anise grows best in rich, well-drained soil with plenty of sunlight. It enjoys a warm climate or a long, hot summer.

+ Start seeds in the spring, outdoors in warm ground or indoors to get a jump on the season. Anise does not transplant well, so move seedlings outdoors while they are still small.

+ Water anise when the soil becomes dry; do not over-water.

+ Keep weed-free and support the stems by mounding dirt around the base if necessary.

+ Harvest flowers in bloom for garnishing. Harvest the frilly lower green leaves throughout the season by snipping them from the main stalk. For seed harvest, cut stems at the base after seeds have formed and begun to mature.

Purchasing tips

Aniseed and anise extract are the most widely available forms of anise and are found in the spice aisle of most grocery stores. If purchasing dried plants or flower heads, make sure they contain seeds.

Storage & preservation tips

* To dry aniseed in a cool, low-moisture location, extract the seeds from the dead flower heads and place them on a baking sheet, or hang stems seed-downward in a secured paper bag. Once dried, store the seeds in an airtight container for up to 2 years.
* To make ground aniseed, crush the seeds in a spice grinder or use a mortar and pestle to make a coarse yellowish powder. Crush the seeds just before use.
* To dry anise leaves, place rinsed, fresh leaves on a paper towel in a cool, dry location. Store the dried leaves in an airtight container in a cool, dark location for up to 12 months.

Try it this way

* Anise seeds can be used in place of caraway seeds in many recipes.
* Toss a few fresh anise leaves with other greens to add distinct flavor to a salad.
* Make a unique fruit salad by mixing diced cantaloupe and blackberries with a few chopped fresh anise leaves; drizzle with 1 to 2 tablespoons orange juice.
* Stir crushed or whole aniseed into cookie or pastry dough before baking.

Special note

There is much confusion surrounding the name 'anise'. Most is due to a completely different plant sharing the same name and a similar flavor; star anise. The anise described above is related to parsley, while star anise is related to the magnolia and comes from an evergreen tree that reaches heights of 60 feet. Star anise is used whole or ground in many Asian dishes and in Chinese five-spice powder. Additionally, a different plant named anise hyssop shares the name, and sweet cicely and fennel are also referred to as anise.

Arugula

What is it?

Often mistaken as lettuce greens, arugula is an annual herb known by various names: rocket, roquette, rochetta, rugula and rucola. Arugula is a member of the mustard family and is native to the Mediterranean region, especially Italy. The plant grows up to 3 feet tall, with edible smooth, wavy, dark green leaves that resemble dandelion leaves. Arugula is often used raw or cooked for salads, but is gaining popularity in sandwiches, pastas dishes or paired with cheeses and vegetables.

Flavor profile

Arugula is peppery with a slightly nutty, mustard flavor and a bitter sting and aroma. Younger, smaller arugula is milder and less bitter.

Growing & harvesting tips

+ Arugula is simple and quick to grow at home from seed. For continual growth, sow the seeds in successive plantings (approximately every 20 to 30 days) from early spring to fall. They can be started as soon as soil can be worked in the spring. After the seedlings have sprouted, they may need to be thinned.

+ Arugula thrives in cool weather and partial shade from an airy tree (no dense shade) or cloth. The plants are generally fuss-free and require minimal care, though summer heat will cause the plant to shoot up, resulting in a bitter taste and no additional new growth of tender small leaves. Provide water and mulch to retain moisture and a cooler temperature.

- Harvest arugula after about 40 days. Cut the base of each leaf close to the ground. Pick young tender leaves, since larger, older leaves are tougher and bitterer. The leaves also taste bitter when harvested during warmer weather.

Purchasing tips

Arugula is available in the produce aisle of most large grocery stores or in specialty markets year-round, with a peak season of June through December. Select bright-green leaves with no signs of wilting. Various types of arugula may be available: micro arugula has tiny leaves that resemble sprouts and can be used more like an herb; baby arugula leaves are usually 2 to 3 inches long and are the best choice for salad greens; mature arugula is bigger, darker green, much stronger and best used wilted in warm salads; and wild arugula, also known as sylvetta, is similar to regular arugula, but with a sharper flavor.

Storage & preservation tips

- Arugula is highly perishable and should be used within 2 days of harvest or purchase. Refrigerate arugula in a plastic bag with stems wrapped loosely in a barely damp paper towel, or like a bouquet with stems in shallow water and a loose plastic covering. Change water daily.
- Arugula requires thorough washing, a soaking, or even several washings in a row. Wash the leaves and pat or spin-dry the leaves just before serving. If arugula is washed before storing, leftover water can cause wilting.

Try it this way

- Arugula makes a good substitute for watercress, baby spinach, endive and radicchio.
- Steam or cook the fresh leaves like fresh spinach; season with a little butter and light sprinkling of salt.
- Mix baby arugula with salad greens. Arugula also makes a good base salad for grilled shrimp and other seafood.
- Add fresh arugula leaves to a stir-fry late in the preparation to cause just a light wilting of the leaves.
- Use it as an extra pizza topping.
- Sauté fresh arugula and toss it with hot pasta, beans or baby potatoes.

Basil

What is it?

Basil, a native of India and the Middle East, is widely known for its place in the Italian kitchen. A relative of mint and an annual plant, basil has many different varieties ranging from 8 to 36 inches in height, rich green to red purple and smooth to crinkled leaves. The variety most prominently used in Italian cuisine is sweet basil which has small, white flower spikes. While the flowers of basil are edible, it is grown for its flavorful leaves. Basil is said to have grown around Christ's tomb following the resurrection and its name to have derived from Greek, meaning "kingly herb."

Flavor profile

Basil is minty with overtones of cloves and sweet licorice-like flavor. Hints of other flavors such as lemon, thyme or cinnamon are found in individual varieties.

Growing & harvesting tips

+ Basil grows easily from seeds. Use plug trays, rather than seed beds, as basil has a long tap root and dislikes being transplanted. Seedlings can be repotted or moved outdoors once they have developed two pairs of true leaves.

+ Warmth and sunlight are required. Do not expose to frost; plant seeds late in the spring, or start plants indoors.

+ Provide rich, well-drained, moist soil.

+ Harvest basil leaves from the top of the plant when they are young, before the plant flowers. This encourages new growth. Do not let the flower go to seed as that will diminish the flavor.

- Basil is a good garden companion for tomatoes, with complementary flavors and similar growth requirements.

Purchasing tips

Sweet basil is available in the grocery store year-round. Look for fresh, brightly colored, fragrant leaves and firm stems. Avoid wilted, yellowed or blackened leaves. Dried sweet leaf basil is the most readily available variety in spice aisles everywhere. Other varieties of fresh or dried basil, such as Thai, holy or lemon can be found in specialty markets.

Storage & preservation tips

- Place fresh basil leaf stems in water like a bouquet while keeping the leaves dry. Cover loosely with plastic and store at room temperature. Basil leaves may also be layered on paper towels, sealed in a plastic bag and refrigerated in the warmest part of the refrigerator, although this sometimes leads to black spotting.

- Dry whole basil leaves (broken leaves are less flavorful due to the loss of oils) in a dehydrator or by hanging bundles of leaves from their stems. Store dried leaves in an airtight container, away from heat, for up to 12 months.

- Basil can be frozen by placing clean, pat-dried and paper towel wrapped leaves in freezer bags for up to 3 months; or finely chop cleaned leaves, mix with water and freeze in ice cube trays. Pop out frozen cubes and store in a sealed freezer bag or airtight container for up to 6 months.

Try it this way

- Sprinkle thinly sliced basil over pizza or pasta for a burst of color and flavor with an Italian flair.

- Layer basil leaves inside sandwiches in place of lettuce.

- Toss whole or torn leaves on salads for a hint of herbal flavor. An example of a great fresh salad starts with mixed greens topped with layered slices of tomato and fresh water-packed mozzarella; tuck in fresh basil leaves and sprinkle with Kalamata olives, extra-virgin olive oil, and black pepper to taste. Serve well chilled.

- Make homemade pesto with fresh basil, Parmesan or Romano cheese, olive oil, pine nuts or walnuts, garlic and pepper.

- Make a stuffing for chicken by combining ½ cup minced fresh basil leaves, 2 tablespoons olive oil, 2 tablespoons fine dried bread crumbs and 2 cloves minced garlic; stuff 4 split chicken breast halves and bake until done.

Bay Leaves

What is it?

Bay leaves grow on the bay laurel evergreen, also known as sweet bay, true laurel or Greek laurel. Originating in Mediterranean countries where it sometimes reaches 60 feet tall, bay laurel more typically reaches 3 to 10 feet tall. Its elliptically-shaped leaves are flat, pointed, dark green and glossy. Ancient Greeks and Romans crowned victors with wreaths of laurel, while the Italians and English believed laurel leaves brought good fortune. Today, bay leaves are frequently used whole to season soups, stews or other slow cooking recipes.

Flavor profile

Bay leaves are aromatic with a unique robust flavor. They are sometimes described as having green, woody, bitter and astringent characteristics.

Growing & harvesting tips

+ Bay laurel can be slow to start from seed and difficult to grow, as perfect temperature and soil conditions are required. Starting a shrub from a cutting is also challenging as rot often develops before roots are established. Purchasing a young plant from the local nursery may lead to more success.

+ Transplant outdoors in early summer, selecting a sunny location protected from strong winds.

+ Since bay laurel prefers hot weather, it should be grown in containers and moved indoors in regions with freezing temperatures.

- Bay laurel is slow growing and tolerant of being pot bound. Provide well-drained but moist soil.
- Bay laurel lends itself to pruning, training and growing as an ornamental plant.
- Begin harvesting leaves once the plant has grown for several seasons. Pick the large leaves first for strongest flavor.

Purchasing tips

Dried bay leaves are available in the spice aisle of the grocery store. Look for unbroken, firm-looking leaves with some semblance of pale green color. Avoid dull brown leaves, as faded color indicates bitterness. Dried sweet bay laurel is commonly available, but specialty markets may offer varieties with different characteristics. Fresh leaves are rarely available.

Storage & preservation tips

- To dry fresh bay leaves, remove leaves from the branch, cover them with a paper towel, and place books on top to flatten them; or hang small branches in a cool dry location. Dry leaves 48 to 72 hours prior to cooking, as freshly dried leaves have stronger flavor. Longer drying time is required for longer storage life. Store dried bay leaves in airtight containers in a cool, dark location for up to 6 months.
- To make ground bay leaves, finely crush dried leaves with a mortar and pestle or coffee grinder, removing any stem remnants.

Try it this way

- Bay leaf is most effective when left as whole leaves and allowed to simmer or marinate in the recipe for several hours. Overuse of bay leaves can result in a bitter taste. Always remove bay leaves before serving a dish.
- Ground bay leaves are great for use in a spice blend rub.
- Use fresh bay leaves as a garnish.
- Add bay leaves to wreaths or arrangements, or to a bowl of floating candles for a fragrant, attractive centerpiece.

Special note

- Dried bay leaves should never be eaten as even small pieces can cause internal cuts and tears.
- The California bay laurel is generally not considered culinary. Nicknamed the "headache tree," its leaves have been known to cause headaches or nausea when crushed and inhaled or eaten.

Borage

What is it?

Borage is sometimes called "starflower" because of its beautiful deep blue (there is also a white variety), star-shaped blossom. The oval-shaped leaves are dark blue-green but appear silvery due to the white prickly hairs covering them. Borage is an annual which commonly grows 1 to 3 feet tall and has a history traced to the Western Mediterranean. A historical symbol of courage, borage was embroidered along with bees to adorn the scarves of knights.

Flavor Profile

Borage has a cool, fresh cucumber flavor and aroma.

Growing & harvesting tips

+ Borage propagates quickly and easily from seed, but it does not transplant well. Sow in early spring or summer directly in the garden. It self-seeds easily, coming back annually, except in very cold climates.

+ Borage tolerates many soil types and sun or partial shade, but grows best with rich, moist soil and full sun.

+ To protect the plants from blowing over, place them close together for self-support.

+ Place borage near tomatoes, squash or strawberries, as it's an excellent companion plant.

+ Borage will bloom from spring through fall. Remove and discard mature flowers to promote continuous blossoming. Harvest blossoms when they are just fully open.

+ Harvest young, small leaves for eating raw or cooking.

Purchasing tips

Fresh borage is not readily available in stores, but fortunately for those wanting to try their green thumb, seeds are available for gardening. The edible borage flowers, more often than leaves, can be found online or in specialty markets. Look for sparkling blue, wide open blossoms. Borage honey, popular because of its mild taste and light clean aroma, is available in specialty markets and online.

Storage & preservation tips

- Rinse leaves and blossoms in cool water before gently patting dry. Refrigerate with a slightly damp paper towel in a sealed plastic bag for up to 4 days.

- Borage does not dry well but the flowers preserve nicely in ice. Fill an ice cube tray half full with water, freeze and knock out the half-cubes; place 1 blossom in each compartment, place a half-cube on top of each blossom and fill the tray with water to freeze, trapping the flower in the middle of the cube.

- To freeze the leaves, finely chop cleaned leaves, mix with water and freeze in ice cube trays. Pop out frozen cubes and store in a sealed freezer bag or airtight container for up to 6 months.

Try it this way

- Use candied or fresh blossoms to garnish cakes or desserts. To make candied flowers, dilute 2 tsp. meringue powder with 2 T. water and lightly brush all sides of the blossom; sprinkle lightly with superfine sugar, completely coating, and allow to dry on a rack or wax paper for 1 to 2 days before use.

- Serve fresh leaves or flowers as part of a green salad; leaves can be finely chopped to disguise the "prickly" hairs.

- Finely chop leaves and add them to a ground meat mixture with fresh bread crumbs, milk and parmesan for cannelloni filling.

- To make a red, white and blue summer salad, drizzle fresh mozzarella, sliced tomatoes and fresh borage blossoms with a light olive oil dressing.

Special note

- Large amounts of borage can be toxic.
- Fresh leaves may cause contact dermatitis.

Chervil

What is it?

Chervil is an annual herb closely related to parsley and even referred to as "gourmet's parsley". It has delicate and lacy green leaves and tiny silvery-white flower clusters. Chervil is native to Russia and Asia and typically grows 15 to 26 inches tall. Its flavorful leaves are essential in classic French cuisine, imparting fresh flavor to salmon, trout, potatoes, spinach, asparagus and green bean dishes. It is also an important part of the French herb blend called fines herbes, along with tarragon, parsley and chives.

Flavor profile

Fresh chervil is sweet and grassy with a touch of licorice flavor.

Growing & harvesting tips

+ Sow fresh seed in the desired growing location, either in the garden or in a container, as chervil has a long tap root and does not transplant well. If grown indoors, treat chervil as a cut-and-come-again plant; harvest down to an inch high and wait for growth of a new crop.

+ Chervil prefers rich, light, moist but well-drained soil. Provide light, regular morning watering.

+ Unlike most culinary herbs, chervil prefers a cool shaded location with only morning or filtered sun. Heat causes chervil to go to seed quickly so plan on growing it in the spring or late fall. Mulch will help keep the plants cool.

+ Successive plantings extend the harvest.

+ Trim regularly to encourage additional growth.

* Harvest the leaves when they are young, after the plant has reached at least 4 inches tall. As the plant matures, the leaves will turn a purple-bronze color and lose their pungency and taste.

Purchasing tips

Fresh chervil is sometimes available in large grocery stores, specialty markets or farmers' markets. Avoid faded color or brown spotting while looking for sprightly, bright green feathery chervil with a pleasant aroma. Dried chervil is available in most spice aisles, but is less flavorful than fresh. It should be bright green with no sign of yellowing due to exposure to light.

Storage & preservation tips

* Since chervil wilts easily, harvest it as close to preparation time as possible.
* Refrigerate fresh chervil, wrapped in lightly damp paper towels and sealed in a plastic bag, for up to 3 days in the vegetable crisper.
* Successful home-drying of chervil is difficult. Store purchased dried chervil in an airtight container in a dry, dark location for up to 6 months.
* To freeze, finely chop cleaned leaves, mix with water and freeze in ice cube trays. Pop out frozen cubes and store in a sealed freezer bag or airtight container for up to 6 months.

Try it this way

* Sprinkle minced fresh chervil leaves over salads, soups or stews; add them just at the end of cooking so their gentle flavor is not diminished. Chervil is not overpowering, so it can be used generously.
* Use the pretty, delicate leaves of chervil as a garnish or to replace parsley in almost any dish.
* Steam carrots and peas, then lather with soft butter combined with fresh minced chervil, salt and pepper.
* Make beautiful radish sandwich hors d'oeuvres by spreading sliced cocktail rye bread with vegetable cream cheese. Layer 3 thinly sliced radishes on top and gently garnishing with individual leaves of chervil.
* Add fresh chervil to pan juices when making chicken gravy.

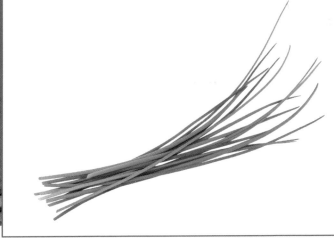

Chives

What is it?

Chives have been around for so long that their specific origin is unknown. They are the only member of the onion group found wild in Europe, Australia and North America. A hardy perennial, with grass-like, bright green, thin and hollow leaves, chives are commonly used as a garnish. The most common variety, sometimes called onion chives, is adorned with purple, globe-shaped flowers and grows 12 to 18 inches tall. Garlic chives are another common variety.

Flavor profile

Chives have a delicate, sweet onion flavor and are refreshingly light. Garlic chives have a garlic tone to their onion flavor.

Growing & harvesting tips

+ Chives are easy to grow and easy to start from seed. Warm temperatures are required for germination, so start indoors in warm seed beds or wait until late spring to sow outdoors. Chives can also be grown from transplants or divisions. Division is required every 2 to 3 years. Lift bulbs in large clumps to divide and replant in 6 to 10 bulb clumps, 6 inches apart, adding fresh compost or manure.

+ While considered generally tolerant, they grow best in a fairly sunny location with rich, well-drained, moist soil. Keep well-watered.

+ Container growth can be successful with generous watering and occasional liquid fertilizer. Forcing bulbs in the winter is also an option; dig bulbs, place in pots for a dormant period in the cold and then bring indoors for growth and harvest through winter.

+ Harvest can begin once chives reach 6 inches tall. Twist a bunch gently and cut with a sharp knife, leaving 1 to 2 inches at the base.

+ Once the chives have finished blooming, cut flower stalks at the soil line and remove them to prevent seeds from forming and to keep the plant productive.

+ Chives can suffer from rust due to fungus. If discovered, cut out diseased growth and burn it. (Do not compost it!)

Purchasing tips

Fresh chives are readily available year-round in large grocery stores. Choose green leaves with uniform size and color and no sign of wilting, yellowing or drying. Less flavorful, freeze-dried chives are available in the spice aisle.

Storage & preservation tips

+ Refrigerate fresh chives in sealed plastic bags for up to 4 days. Rinse with cold water just before use.

+ Successful home-drying of chives is difficult. Store purchased dried chives in an airtight container in a dry, dark location for up to 6 months.

+ To freeze, wash and dry stems completely and wrap in a dry paper towel; or snip chives, mix with water, freeze in ice cube trays and pop out frozen cubes. Store towel-wrapped chives or frozen cubes in an airtight freezer bag or container for up to 6 months.

Try it this way

+ For flavor retention, cut chives with shears rather than a knife and add them near the end of cooking. Small chives have the most crispness. Use chives in place of onions.

+ Use fresh, young flowers to garnish salads or chilled soups, or use chive pieces to garnish appetizers such as deviled eggs.

+ Chives are perfect for tying together small bundles of vegetables or dumplings for a unique presentation.

+ Add snipped chives to coleslaw or potato, tuna or egg salad.

+ Chive butter is great on grilled pork chops or steaks, as well as baked potatoes.

Cilantro (Coriander)

What is it?

Cilantro is a widely used term in the Americas, referring to the small, bright green leaves and stem of the coriander plant. Coriander, the term preferred in the Orient, refers to the whole plant (also called Chinese parsley) and the commonly harvested seeds. Growing up to 24 inches tall, it is a tender annual with white flowers, finely-cut upper leaves, broad scalloped lower leaves and generous seed heads. Coriander, a historical herb originating in Southern Europe and the Middle East, is widely used today in Asian, Caribbean and Latin American cooking.

Flavor profile

Cilantro has an earthy flavor, suggestive of ginger, freshly mown hay and leafy vegetables. Some describe the flavor as bright and citrus-like, while others say it is soapy. Coriander seed is reminiscent of lemon, sage and caraway.

Growing & harvesting tips

+ Sow seeds outdoors in the early spring, or in the late fall for winter growth in a mild, frost-free climate. Propagation in seed or plug trays is not recommended.
+ Plant in light, well-drained soil with partial to full sunlight. A mild, dry climate is preferred. Water regularly to keep soil moist.
+ If planted too late in the season, cilantro can prematurely flower, causing the leaves to become bitter.
+ Stake mature cilantro if it has a weak stem or heavy seed head. Harvest seed heads when they present a pleasant, citrus scent, indicating ripeness.

+ Harvest leaves anytime plants are at least 6 inches tall
  and bright green.

Purchasing tips

Fresh cilantro is available year-round in large grocery stores
and specialty markets. Look for bright green, aromatic
leaves without yellow coloring or wilting. Freeze-dried
cilantro is sometimes available, but will usually lack the
color and flavor of fresh. Whole and ground coriander seed
are in the spice aisle.

Storage & preservation tips

+ Wrap fresh stems with a wet paper towel or place stem
  ends directly in water, covering leaves loosely with a plastic
  bag. Refrigerate for up to 1 week, changing water every
  1 to 2 days.
+ Although there is limited success in preserving the flavor of
  cilantro, freezing provides better results than drying. Place
  individual leaves on a cookie sheet and freeze. Transfer
  them to a sealed bag and return to the freezer for up to 6
  months.
+ Store purchased freeze-dried cilantro in a cool, dark
  location for up to 12 months or until scent fades.
+ To dry coriander seeds, place stems, with seed heads
  downward, into a paper bag. Secure the bag tightly to hang
  in a dry, warm and airy location for 10 days. Seeds will
  come away from hulls easily. Store in an airtight container
  for up to 2 years.
+ Since ground coriander quickly loses flavor, toast and grind
  dry seeds just before use.

Try it this way

+ Cilantro leaves should be used raw or added to dishes late
  in the cooking process, as flavor fades quickly when cooked.
+ Add freshly chopped cilantro to guacamole or fresh salsa.
  Use whole leaves to garnish soups, chili or burritos.
+ Stir a handful of chopped cilantro into jasmine rice with
  chopped peanuts, or mix it with melted butter for grilled
  chicken or corn.
+ Coriander seeds are often used in pickling, relishes and
  curries. Toast seeds in a dry frying pan on low heat
  for the most flavor.

Dill

What is it?

Dill is known for the use of its fine, feathery green leaves and flat, oval-shaped brown seeds in pickling and seasoning vegetables and fishes. Native to Europe and Western Asia, dill is popular in Greek, Polish, Russian and Scandinavian cuisine. It is an annual which reaches heights of 5 feet with flat clusters of tiny yellow-green flowers and umbrella-shaped seed heads. Dried and fresh dill leaves, as well as the entire plant, are sometimes referred to as dillweed.

Flavor profile

Dill has a delicate, refreshing flavor reminiscent of parsley and anise with a fragrant lemony aroma. Dill seed has a tangy flavor that is stronger than the leaves.

Growing & harvesting tips

+ Start seeds in the garden or indoors in plug trays. Plant outdoors when the soil and air has started to warm. Transplant seedlings when they are just large enough to handle since they don't like to move. Successive planting is recommended.

+ Dill prefers full sun and rich, well-drained soil. Provide plenty of water during hot summers.

+ Dill needs room to grow tall and wide. Do not plant dill near caraway, fennel or angelica due to cross-pollination potential.

+ Protect dill from wind, tying up with supports if necessary.

+ Begin to harvest stems once the plant reaches 6 inches tall, continuing until seed heads form.

- Harvest seed stalks when seeds begin to darken, indicating ripeness. Dill easily self-seeds; do not compost seed heads.

Purchasing tips

Fresh dill is widely available in the produce aisle of most grocery stores. Look for feathery, fernlike, deep green leaves that are not wet, slimy or extremely wilted. Minor wilting is acceptable as dill droops quickly after picking. Dried dill and whole seed are available in spice aisles.

Storage & preservation tips

- Store fresh dill in the refrigerator for up to 3 days; loosely wrap it in a barely damp paper towel and plastic, or set stems in shallow water and cover loosely with plastic.
- Successful home-drying of dill is difficult. Store purchased dried dill in an airtight container in a dry, dark location for up to 6 months.
- To freeze, finely chop cleaned leaves, mix with water and freeze in ice cube trays. Pop out frozen cubes and store in a sealed freezer bag or airtight container for up to 2 months.
- To dry seeds, place the head of seed stalks downward into a paper bag, tie shut and hang in a cool, dry location. Seeds dry in about 1 week and should separate easily from the hull. Store dried seeds in an airtight container for up to 6 months.

Try it this way

- Seeds can be used ground or whole, fresh leaves should be chopped or torn, and dried leaves should be crushed. Leaves lose flavor with heat, while seeds increase flavor with heat.
- Use dill to season fish, soft cheeses, salads, omelets or vegetable dishes like carrots, spinach, beets and potatoes.
- To make warm green bean salad, steam 2 pounds trimmed green beans until tender and toss with a blended dressing of 2 tablespoons cider vinegar, ⅓ cup olive oil, 2 teaspoons dill seeds and ¼ cup chopped fresh dill. Salt and pepper to taste.
- Make dill butter with ¼ cup minced fresh dill and ½ cup soft butter and refrigerate for at least 2 hours before serving with seafood or savory breads.

Fennel

What is it?

There are two main types of fennel. Common fennel produces the familiar oval, greenish-brown seeds used in seasoning meats. Florence fennel (finocchio) is a celery-like plant with a bulbous base eaten as a vegetable. While common fennel is a perennial and Florence fennel is an annual, both are treated as annuals in colder climates. Common fennel grows 3 to 6 feet tall and Florence fennel only reaches about 2 feet tall. Both varieties have yellow flowers and present flavorful, bright green feathery foliage (resembling dill) used as a seasoning herb.

Flavor profile

Fennel is aromatic with a warm anise or sweet licorice-like flavor.

Growing & harvesting tips

+ Sow seeds directly in the garden.
+ Fennel prefers full sun and well-drained fertilized soil. Water Florence fennel regularly. Common fennel requires watering while taking root, but withstands dry conditions when mature.
+ Harvest Florence fennel bulbs when tennis ball size or bigger. Thin bulbs if necessary. Harvest common fennel foliage once the plant is at least 6 inches tall, taking only the top 2 inches for continued growth.
+ Harvest seeds of common fennel as soon as they turn from green to brown. Wrap seed heads with cheesecloth or snap off into a paper bag.

- Avoid planting fennel near beans, caraway, tomatoes, dill or coriander. Common fennel can become invasive and is sometimes considered a weed. To contain, remove ripe seed or flower heads and discard properly. (Do not compost!)

Purchasing tips

While Florence fennel is available in the produce aisle of large grocery stores, common fennel is a challenge to find. Florence fennel should be firm and unblemished with plump creamy white bulbs, crisp glossy stalks and bright green foliage. Avoid flowered Florence fennel since it is too mature. It is sometimes incorrectly labeled as anise. Whole fennel seed, and occasionally dried fennel leaves, are available in the spice aisle.

Storage & preservation tips

- Wrap Florence fennel tightly in plastic to refrigerate for up to 4 or 5 days. Wash just before use. Sprinkle cut Florence fennel with lemon juice to prevent discoloration.

- Because the frilly foliage of fennel wilts quickly, snip just before use if possible. For short-term refrigeration, place stems in water like a bouquet and cover the top with loose plastic.

- To dry the seeds of common fennel, remove seed heads as soon as they turn from green to brown, placing them in a paper bag. Dry completely in a dark location before storing seeds in an airtight container for up to 6 months.

- To freeze the fennel leaves for up to 6 months, wash and dry stems completely before stripping leaves. Place leaves directly into a freezer bag, or freeze them with water in ice cube trays, pop out frozen cubes and place them in a freezer bag. Store for up to 6 months.

Try it this way

- Prepare Florence fennel like celery; discard any bruised or discolored outer layers along with a small slice from the bottom of the bulb. It can be sautéed, stewed, braised, grilled or eaten raw.

- Serve Florence fennel on a relish tray in place of celery.

- Toss wet stalks and leaves on the grill in lieu of wood chips.

- Use the frilly foliage or edible flowers to make a beautiful garnish.

- Chopped fennel leaves are often eaten with oily fish such as salmon. Mix ¼ cup butter, 2 teaspoons lemon juice, 2 tablespoons chopped fennel leaves and a dash of salt and pepper to make a delicious butter for fish.

Garlic

What is it?

Garlic is a small plant with a big reputation for a special taste like nothing else. Native to India and Central Asia, garlic has a long history and is essential in dishes around the world today. A perennial, mainly grown as an annual, the garlic plant reaches 16 to 24 inches in height and produces purple flowers and a bulb with an average size of 2 inches. The useful bulb divides into segments (cloves) covered with a white paper-like skin.

Flavor profile

Garlic's unique flavor is hot and pungent but shadowed by a subtle sweetness. With a reputation for its strong odor, it is sometimes called the "stinking rose."

Growing & harvesting tips

+ Propagate by planting bulbs in early fall (after killing frost) to early spring. Split the bulbs just before planting the individual cloves, point upward, 1 inch deep and 6 inches apart. A healthy root develops before it goes dormant. Leafy shoots develop in the spring. A light layer of mulch retains moisture, deters weeds and protects during cold spells.

+ Grow in full sun with rich, light and well-drained soil. Water garlic through growth periods, but cut back watering when it begins to ripen.

+ Remove flower stalks (which only develop in warm climates) so the plant can focus energy on bulb development.

- Garlic can be grown in a container in a sunny, springtime window. Snip green shoots to use like chives and harvest the smaller than normal bulbs in the summer.
- Harvest garlic when top growth loses color and shoots die back. Test one bulb to see if it is large, firm and ripe before easing bulbs from the ground and brushing off soil.

Purchasing tips

Fresh garlic bulbs are available year-round in grocery stores. Look for firm, plump bulbs with dry skins; avoid soft, shriveled and refrigerated ones. Prepared garlic such as paste, crushed, minced or whole cloves in jars or tubes are widely available. Find dried garlic in the spice aisle as dehydrated flakes (reconstitute unless preparing in liquid dishes) or ground as powder.

Storage & preservation tips

- Dry whole fresh garlic bulbs in the sun for 3 to 4 days. Braid foliage to hang a string of bulbs or trim foliage to 1 inch to hang bulbs in a net-bag. Store garlic bulbs in a cool, dark, airy location. Inspect regularly and remove dried-out, soft, moldy or sprouting bulbs. Do not refrigerate bulbs or store them with other food.
- Once cloves have been separated from the bulb, store remaining portions in a sealed plastic bag for up to 8 days.
- Store purchased prepared garlic in the refrigerator for up to 3 months or according to manufacturer's instructions.

Try it this way

- Apply pressure to whole bulbs to break cloves (segments) away. Gently crush or pound the clove to loosen the paper-like skin for removal. Crushing, chopping, pressing or pureeing garlic cloves releases the oils for flavor.
- The longer garlic is cooked, the milder the flavor.
- Puree fresh garlic with canned garbanzo beans, tahini (crushed sesame seeds), olive oil and lemon juice to make hummus dip.
- Mash roasted garlic with cooked potatoes and olive oil.

Special note

- Never store garlic in oil at room temperature as it is a prime breeding ground for botulism.

Ginger

What is it?

Ginger is a perennial rhizome, meaning it has an underground stem from which shoots grow upward and roots grow downward. The useful stem, commonly called gingerroot because of its below-ground position, is thick and knobby with smooth beige skin and flesh that ranges from pale greenish-yellow to ivory. Ginger is native to Asia, where it is still essential in many dishes and curries. Ground ginger is commonly used in European and American baked goods.

Flavor profile

Ginger is peppery and slightly sweet with a rich, spicy aroma.

Growing & harvesting tips

+ Ginger enjoys a tropical climate with temperatures over 85°F, lots of water, rich soil and a long growing season.

+ Adventurous gardeners in non-tropical regions should try container gardening. Ginger is most commonly started through cuttings. The best source for a cutting is a fresh root from the grocery store, with at least one hearty-looking bud. Slice the root 2 inches below the bud and plant just below the surface of well-drained soil with the bud facing up. Water sparingly at first and more generously after sprouting. Provide a large container for horizontal growth, a warm indoor location and regular "misting" with water.

Purchasing tips

Ginger comes in many forms. Fresh mature ginger is available in the produce aisle of many grocery stores while fresh young ginger, sometimes called spring ginger, is available in Asian markets. Either way, select fresh ginger with smooth (not wrinkled) skin and no sign of mold. Ground ginger is available in spice aisles everywhere. Other forms of ginger are less commonly available, but can be ordered online or found in specialty markets. Dried whole ginger is either 'black' (with the skin left on) or 'white' (with the skin peeled off) and must be soaked in water for 1 hour to re-hydrate before use. Pickled pink or red ginger, known as 'gari' in Japan, is often served alongside sushi as a palate cleanser. Preserved ginger, with sugar and salt, is generally added to desserts. Crystallized ginger, 'candied' in sugar syrup and granulated sugar, is commonly used in desserts or as a snack. Finally, ginger juice is liquid pressed from roots and substituted for ginger in various recipes.

Storage & preservation tips

+ Fresh ginger should be stored unpeeled and wrapped tightly in a paper towel and plastic; refrigerate for up to 3 weeks or freeze for up to 3 months.

+ Store dried or ground ginger in an airtight container in a cool, dark location for up to 12 months.

+ Pickled, preserved, crystallized ginger and ginger juice should be refrigerated following the instructions provided on the original packaging.

Try it this way

+ Ground ginger is quite different from fresh, so substitution is generally not recommended.

+ Fresh gingerroot should be peeled and cut into chunks or grated for recipes.

+ Dip crystallized ginger into chocolate for an exotic snack.

+ Make ginger ice cream by finely grating a 2½-inch piece of fresh peeled ginger and pressing it through a fine sieve, using the back of a spoon to get the most juice possible. Fold the juice into 1 pint of softened vanilla ice cream, refreeze it until firm and garnish with a piece of crystallized ginger.

+ Make creamy peanut ginger dip by combining a 1-inch cube of peeled ginger, 1 cup peanut butter, ¼ cup soy sauce, 1 clove garlic, 6 tablespoons apple cider vinegar and ¼ cup roughly chopped cilantro in a food processor. Pulse for 20 seconds while gradually adding ¼ cup hot water. Serve with crisp raw vegetables or breads, or over warm noodles.

Horseradish

What is it?

Horseradish, a perennial, is a large-leaved native herb of Europe, where it has long been paired with beef. It is grown mainly for the firm, white flesh of its long brownish-skinned tap root, which reaches 2 feet in length. Above ground, the plant reaches 2 to 3 feet tall with small white flowers which generally produce sterile seeds. Horseradish's volatile, mustard-like oil brings tears to the eyes and heat to the tongue, generally resulting in rapture or repulsion for those who taste it.

Flavor profile

Horseradish has a sharp, hot, almost burning taste and sensory effect.

Growing & harvesting tips

+ Propagate in early spring by root cutting or division; cut 6-inch pieces of root and replant at 45° angles, all in the same direction. If existing horseradish is unavailable, seek plants through a nursery or garden center.

+ A sunny location with deep, well-dug, rich, moist soil is preferred. Prepare the ground in the fall with well-rotted manure; fresh manure can cause excessive top growth and forked roots. Roots can also be malformed and yields reduced by hard, shallow or rocky soils.

+ Mulch for weed control and moisture retention.

+ Horseradish is highly invasive; be sure to collect all little pieces of root while working with it.

+ Root growth is greatest during late summer and early fall, so delay harvest until just before the ground freezes. Dig roots for winter storage and use. If the horseradish patch is mature, roots can be dug for use anytime.

Purchasing tips

Fresh horseradish root is available in the produce aisle of large grocery stores or specialty markets. Choose firm roots without sign of blemish, mold, green spots or withering. Jars or bottles of preserved horseradish or creamy horseradish sauces are widely available in grocery stores. Powdered root, which must be reconstituted before use, is available in specialty markets or online.

Storage & preservation tips

+ Freshly dug roots should be buried in a container of sand, and kept cold (32° to 40°F) for long-term storage.

+ For short-term storage, wrap fresh horseradish roots tightly in plastic and place in a paper bag to refrigerate. Protect from light to prevent them from turning green. Store purchased roots for 1 to 2 weeks and homegrown roots for 3 to 4 weeks. Wash and peel fresh roots just before use.

+ To preserve horseradish with vinegar, scrub and peel roots, chop, add a little water and pulse in a food processor or blender until well-ground. Strain water and add 3 tablespoons white vinegar and ½ teaspoon salt for each cup of grated horseradish. The vinegar causes a chemical reaction which will stabilize its degree of hotness. Chopped horseradish is very potent, so process in a well-ventilated area. Refrigerate for 3 to 4 weeks in a covered jar and discard when color darkens.

Try it this way

+ Horseradish root is rarely cooked, as the heat diminishes the aroma and flavor.

+ Young leaves can be added to a green salad.

+ Use homegrown prepared horseradish in homemade shrimp cocktail sauce.

+ Make creamy horseradish sauce for beef by combining ½ cup mayonnaise, ½ cup prepared horseradish, 2 tablespoons Dijon mustard, ⅛ teaspoon sugar, ¼ teaspoon salt and ¼ teaspoon pepper and blending well; slowly whisk in ¾ cup whipping cream to desired consistency.

+ Add prepared horseradish to deviled eggs or meatloaf for a new twist on a classic.

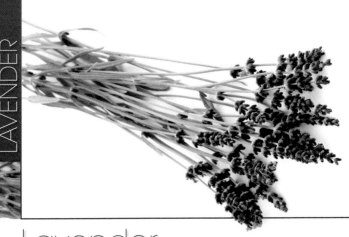

Lavender

What is it?

Lavender is a perennial often recognized for the beauty and fragrance of its flowers, rather than its culinary benefits. English lavender, also known as true lavender, is the most widely-used culinary version due to its sweet, mild taste. Growing 1½ to 3 feet tall, lavender's narrow, silver-green leaves and purple flowers that bloom on long spikes are aromatic and edible. It is a native of the Mediterranean, Canary Isles and India, but is now widely popular in "country" gardens.

Flavor profile

Lavender has a sweet floral flavor with hints of lemon and citrus.

Growing & harvesting tips

+ Lavender is difficult and slow to start from seed, so propagation by cutting is recommended. Cut a fresh shoot that includes an older piece of the existing plant and place in well-drained soil.

+ Warm, sunny climates are best, so grow lavender in containers with protection through the winter in cold climates. Plant in equal parts soil-based compost and composted fine bark. Feed with liquid fertilizer through the flowering stage, and allow the pot to mostly dry out during the winter.

+ Watering is especially important for lavender in arid conditions or if grown in pots.

+ To maintain lavender, trim in the spring and before danger of frost in the fall. Don't cut into the old wood, as it will not re-shoot. After flowering, trim stems back to the leaves.

- Harvest flowers just as they open. Select the freshest blossoms with the fullest color. Pick the leaves any time for fresh use or before flowering for drying.

Purchasing tips

Dried lavender is available in health food or specialty markets (often displayed with tea-making supplies) or online. Culinary fresh lavender is difficult to find, but may be available at farmers' markets or specialty markets. Always purchase lavender from reliable sources that is clearly labeled for culinary use. Do not eat lavender from florists, nurseries or garden centers as it has often been treated with chemicals or pesticides not safe for consumption.

Storage & preservation tips

- Although fresh lavender is best when used upon harvest, it can be stored at room temperature by placing the stems in water like a floral bouquet.

- Before using or drying blossoms, immerse in cool water to flush out any insects or soil.

- To dry lavender, hang bundles upside-down in a well-ventilated, dry, cool, dark location for approximately 2 weeks, or dry on trays. Store dried buds in an airtight container in a cool, dry location for up to 6 months.

- To preserve lavender flavor in sugar, bury blossoms in sugar, store in an airtight container for 2 weeks, then discard the lavender before using the sugar in ordinary recipes.

Try it this way

- Lavender flowers and buds (or even leaves) can be used fresh or dried; flavor beverages, baked goods and fruit soups, as well as less traditional dishes like beef.

- Add lavender sparingly, as it is potent; too much is like eating perfume. If using dried lavender in place of fresh, use only one-third of the amount.

- To make a pepper-rub for tenderloin, grind 2 tablespoons dried lavender with 2 tablespoons whole peppercorns, 2 tablespoons fennel seed and 2 teaspoons dried thyme.

- Add 1 tablespoon of crumbled fresh lavender flowers to your favorite butter cookie recipe.

- Use fresh lavender petals to garnish soup, salad, chocolate cake, champagne or ice cream.

- Make potpourri or a linen sachet. Lavender repels insects like moths and flies.

Lemongrass

What is it?

Lemongrass is a tender perennial that reaches heights of
6 feet in tropical regions and 3 feet in Northern regions.
This tropical grass grows as a dense clump of white bulbs,
extending to thick, yellow-green, fleshy shoots and tall reed-
like grayish-green leaves. Lemongrass is native to India and
is widely used in Thai and other Southeast Asian cuisine.

Flavor profile

Lemongrass has a subtle citrus flavor with hints of ginger
and a fresh lemony scent.

Growing & harvesting tips

+ Lemongrass enjoys a long hot summer with full sun, heat,
  plenty of water, sandy soil and a good layer of mulch.

+ Seeds or potted seedlings are sometimes available; however,
  the most successful way to grow lemongrass is by cutting or
  division from a host plant. Detach one or more bulbs, place
  in a container of moist sand for plant establishment and
  later transplant outdoors in warm temperatures.

+ An alternate propagation method is through purchased
  fresh lemongrass with roots remaining. Place it in water
  until healthy roots and additional growth have formed
  before transplanting.

+ In non-tropic climates, lemongrass plants should be cut
  back to 4 to 8 inch stubs, dug, and potted for protected
  storage prior to a killing frost. In warm climates (night
  temperature above 48°F), it can be left outdoors through
  the winter and pruned of old growth in the spring.

- Lemongrass makes an excellent container plant. Keep it moist through the growing season. Cut it back, reduce watering and allow it to go dormant in a cool area during the winter.
- To harvest lemongrass, snap off shoots from the outer edge of the base, near the root.
- Lemongrass makes a nice contrasting backdrop for shorter flowers or herbs.

Purchasing tips

Fresh lemongrass is available in specialty and ethnic markets or large grocery stores. Look for firm, blemish-free green stalks with white bulbs which are not rubbery, dry or brittle. Dried or ground forms of lemongrass for use in teas and curries are available, but are not a good substitute when fresh is called for. Prepared, ready-to-use lemongrass may also be purchased in the frozen section of ethnic markets.

Storage & preservation tips

- Tightly wrap whole fresh lemongrass in plastic and refrigerate for up to 2 weeks. Its flavor can easily be imparted to other foods during storage.
- Prepare fresh lemongrass for use (see below) and freeze it in a sealed freezer bag for up to 5 months.

Try it this way

- Cut off and discard the lower end of the bulb and remove tough outer leaves. Cut the lower 5 to 6 inches into pieces. Just before use, crush them with the side of a chef's knife or pound lightly with a kitchen mallet to release the flavor. The upper portions of the stems can be used to flavor soups and curries. Remove any pieces of lemongrass, or warn guests of their inclusion, as they are inedible.
- To brew lemongrass and ginger tea, place 1 stalk of sliced lemongrass and ¼ cup freshly minced gingerroot in 1 quart water and simmer gently for 10 minutes; remove from heat and steep 2 bags of tea with the mixture; strain and sweeten with honey and lemon to taste.
- Mince small pieces of lemongrass for a marinade along with soy sauce, garlic and lemon-lime soda.
- Line foil with crushed stalks before adding meats and vegetables for grilling.
- Tie several blades of lemongrass stem together to lie across baking fish to diminish the "fishy" smell or taste.

Lemon Verbena

What is it?

Lemon verbena is a tropical herb which originated in Chile. Its wonderful fragrance is memorable, making it a favorite of many including Scarlet O'Hara's mother in the movie "Gone with the Wind." This woody perennial shrub has slender apple-green leaves and sprays of tiny white flowers. It grows up to 15 feet tall in the tropics, but more commonly grows 3 to 4 feet in height.

Flavor profile

Lemon Verbena has a sharp scent and is reminiscent of lemon candy with its sweet, strong lemon flavor.

Growing & harvesting tips

+ Since seeds are slow to germinate, purchase plants or start with cuttings. Provide new cuttings and the original plant with shade and plenty of water as protection from wilting.

+ Plant in full sun with rich, free-draining and warm soil. Keep moist but not soggy.

+ For container growing, select a pot at least 8 inches in diameter. Provide equal parts of soil-based compost and composted fine bark. Provide liquid fertilizer during the flowering stage and water well. Keep lemon verbena in pots for the first 2 years.

+ As a tropical plant, lemon verbena prefers a warm, humid climate, with protection from temperatures below 40°F. It grows in colder climates with extra care. Move it into a cool protected area during the winter. Allow it to become dormant, drop its leaves and nearly dry out. Move lemon verbena outdoors in the springtime, watering it and cutting back the old growth after new growth appears.

+ Cut the top of the main stem regularly to promote branching for a fuller-formed plant. Cut off blossoms once the flowering process is complete.

+ Harvest leaves throughout the growing season after the plant has grown at least 1 foot tall.

Purchasing tips

Fresh lemon verbena is sometimes found in large grocery stores or specialty markets during hot summer months. Look for fresh, bright-colored and fragrant leaves. Dried lemon verbena is available in specialty stores.

Storage & preservation tips

+ Fresh leaves wilt quickly, so store for minimal time in the refrigerator, wrapped in damp paper towels inside a plastic bag.

+ Leaves dry quickly and easily while holding their color and scent. Spread leaves on screens or hang sprigs in a dry location. A quick alternative method is to place leaves on a parchment-lined cookie sheet in the oven with the oven light on. It will provide just enough heat to dry the leaves within a few days. Store in an airtight container for up to 12 months.

Try it this way

+ Leaves can be tough so they may need to be removed before serving dishes.

+ Flavor oil, vinegar, drinks, desserts, jellies, cakes or fish with fresh leaves.

+ Add a teaspoon of fresh chopped lemon verbena leaves to homemade ice cream for a delicious dessert.

+ Enhance lemonade with fresh leaves or steep tea with dry ones.

+ Add finely crumbled dried leaves to the batters of carrot, banana or zucchini bread.

+ Make lavender and lemon verbena dip by mixing 8 ounces softened cream cheese, 8 ounces sour cream, ½ cup finely chopped lemon verbena leaves, 1 teaspoon (culinary) lavender buds, ¼ cup fresh squeezed lemon juice and ¼ cup sugar; chill overnight and serve with slices of fruit or cookies.

+ Make fresh potpourri or linen sachets with lemon verbena leaves.

Lovage

What is it?

Lovage is a perennial herb which grows in a tall clump with rigid, hollow stems. It has glossy, bright-green, celery-like leaves and greenish-yellow flower heads with tiny flowerets. A native of the Mediterranean, it now grows wild in many locations. The stems, seeds, leaves and roots can all be used for culinary purposes. Lovage, sometimes called "love parsley", grows full and up to 6 feet tall at maturity, making it an excellent backdrop in the garden.

Flavor profile

Lovage has a potent celery flavor with a hint of anise and a warm, spicy fragrance.

Growing & harvesting tips

+ Lovage can be propagated by division or easily by seed. Sow fresh seeds outdoors in the late summer or fall, or indoors in extremely cold climates (moving outdoors in early spring). When seedlings are large enough, replant with a 2 to 3 foot separation.

+ Rich, moist but well-drained soil and partial to full sun is preferred.

+ To maintain, apply an organic fertilizer annually, water regularly and divide after several years.

+ To harvest, cut stems from the outside of the plant, leaving the center intact. Leaves are mild and tender early in the season.

+ Harvest the seed head after seeds have begun to ripen and turn brown. Do not allow the plants to drop seeds or many unwanted saplings could result.

Purchasing tips

Fresh lovage is not readily available for purchase. Chopped or powdered stalks or root are sometimes available in health food stores or gourmet markets.

Storage & preservation tips

+ Use fresh lovage leaves straight from the herb garden rather than attempting to store for fresh or dried use.

+ To dry seeds, hang stems seed-downward in a secured paper bag, in an airy location for several weeks. Store dried seed in an airtight container for up to 2 years in a cool, dry, dark location.

+ To blanch and freeze lovage, rinse leaves, drop briefly into boiling water, dip in an ice bath for 1 to 2 minutes and drain. Chop leaves, mix with water and freeze in ice cube trays. Pop out frozen cubes and store in a sealed freezer bag or airtight container for up to 6 months.

Try it this way

+ Lovage can be overpowering, so use it sparingly. When making a substitution for celery, use half the recommended amount. It can be coarse or fibrous, so chop leaves finely and blanch stems to tenderize.

+ Use lovage to season slow-cooked dishes, especially those including potatoes, peas, beans or lentils.

+ Use the pretty, leafy straw as a garnish or to stir a Bloody Mary.

+ Lovage seed can flavor sour pickles and aromatic vinegars.

+ Use candied lovage stems to adorn cakes or desserts.

+ Make lovage sauce to serve over pork. Melt 2 tablespoons butter and sauté 12 minced lovage leaves for about 3 minutes; simmer for another minute after adding 2 tablespoons dry white wine. Stir in 1 teaspoon Dijon mustard and season with salt and pepper.

Special note

+ Due to medical risk, large amounts of lovage should not be consumed if suffering from kidney problems, menstrual disorders or if pregnant.

+ Be sure to grow a lovage variety that is intended for consumption, as some varieties are poisonous.

Marjoram

What is it?

Marjoram (sweet marjoram) is a close relative of oregano (wild marjoram). It is sometimes known as knotted marjoram due to tiny white flowers that appear as knots. Although similar to oregano, the two herbs are actually quite distinct, with marjoram being sweeter and milder. Marjoram has square woody stems, round pale green opposite leaves and whorled flower spikes. A half-hardy perennial often grown as an annual, it generally reaches 12 inches in height. Originating in North Africa, it was introduced to Europe in the 16th century. Marjoram is an important flavor in German sausages and is often used in French, Italian and Portuguese cooking.

Flavor profile

Marjoram has a delicate minty-sweet flavor with the aroma of freshly mown hay.

Growing & harvesting tips

+ Marjoram grows easily from seed, but will grow from cuttings as well. Provide evenly moist soil during germination.

+ Cultivate in sandy soil with partial to full sun; plant or transplant outdoors after danger of frost has passed.

+ Marjoram works well for container gardening, indoors or out. Plenty of room to breathe is needed, so do not overcrowd. Marjoram can winter indoors; allow the soil to dry, but not dry out, between waterings.

+ Pinch back tops of plants to promote bushy growth.

- Harvesting can begin after plants reach 6 inches in height. To catch flavor at its peak, snip sprigs just after flowers have budded but not yet bloomed.

Purchasing tips

Marjoram can be grown hydroponically, so it can be found fresh year-round in specialty markets or large grocery stores. When fresh, it should have good color and a fresh, clean scent. Avoid any brown spots or wilted leaves or stalks. Dried leaf or ground marjoram is readily available in spice aisles.

Storage & preservation tips

- Fresh marjoram is highly perishable, so purchase only as needed. For short-term storage, immerse freshly cut stems in 2 inches of water, cover leaves loosely with plastic and refrigerate for up to 3 days.

- The flavor of marjoram becomes more intense when dried. Hang bunches of marjoram or spread sprigs on a screen to dry in a warm, dark location. Store in an airtight container for up to 6 months.

- Freeze sprigs on a cookie sheet. Once frozen, strip the leaves (discard the stem) and freeze them for up to 2 months in freezer bags or airtight containers.

Try it this way

- Marjoram is excellent for seasoning beef, pork, chicken, stuffings, tomatoes, salad dressings and chowders.

- Bake a fully cooked bone-in ham with 2½ cups Madeira wine and 1 cup orange juice until heated through (about 45 minutes) at 400°F. Remove from oven, increase temperature to 450°F and spread the following mixture generously on the ham: 1½ cups Dijon mustard, ½ cup brown sugar, 3 tablespoons dried marjoram, 2 tablespoons minced garlic, 2 tablespoons orange juice concentrate and 1 teaspoon ground black pepper. Return to the oven until coating is golden brown (about 35 minutes).

- Harvest flowers for use in salads.

- Try adding 2 tablespoons of minced marjoram to a cornbread recipe or minestrone.

- Marjoram's delightful fragrance is perfect for a sachet in a linen drawer or potpourri.

Mint

What is it?

Mint is a widely-used herb with numerous varieties including orange, lemon, apple and even chocolate mint. The two most prominent culinary mints are peppermint and spearmint, which generally grow up to 2 feet tall with oval-shaped, serrated rich-green leaves. According to Greek mythology, mint was originally a nymph transformed into a plant by the jealous Goddess Persephone. The origin of mint is traced to the Mediterranean, but it is now grown around the world.

Flavor profile

Mint has a clean, refreshing taste and range of aromas. Peppermint is aggressive with peppery flavor, while spearmint has a milder cooling flavor.

Growing & harvesting tips

+ Mint grows best by division or stem cuttings. Cut a sprig from an existing plant at least 2 inches below a leaf joint with 3 to 4 pairs of leaves. Remove the lower leaves up to the most fully developed pair, and gently plant the base of the stem with the bare lower leaf joints buried. Water regularly and transplant it when new roots are established.

+ Rich, moist, well-drained soil and partial to full sun are preferred. Light mulch retains moisture and keeps leaves clean.

+ Mint is easy to grow and spreads quickly with underground runners. Plant mint inside a bottomless container which has been buried at least 12 inches deep to prevent proliferation.

- Mint likes container gardening and can be forced indoors through the winter. Dig up roots in the fall and replant mint in pots for continuous indoor harvest.
- Harvest fresh leaves throughout the season by snipping the tops of plants. Tips with small leaves are sweetest and should be reserved for garnishing. Harvest leaves for drying before the plant flowers.

Purchasing tips

Fresh mint is available seasonally at farmers' markets and year-round in many grocery stores. Select mint with uniform green coloring and no wilting. Dried mint and mint extract are available in most spice aisles, while mint oil is found in specialty markets or online.

Storage & preservation tips

- Refrigerate mint with stems placed in water and leaves covered with plastic for up to 1 week. Change water daily.
- To prevent mold, speed-dry mint by baking clean leaves for 2 to 4 hours at 180°F until crumbly. Store dried leaves in an airtight container for up to 12 months in the freezer.
- Freeze individual fresh leaves on trays, transferring them to an airtight container for freezer storage for up to 6 months.

Try it this way

- Fresh mint is used to season savory dishes, such as lamb, or sweet dishes, such as chilled soups, fruit salads or chocolate. Dried leaves are commonly used in Middle Eastern dishes like yogurt dips, sauces or tea. Oils and extracts are used in cookies or candies.
- Crush mint leaves and fold into whipped cream for a chocolate dessert topping.
- To make chilled strawberry-mint soup, combine 1½ cups fresh sliced strawberries, ¾ cup sour cream, ¾ cup heavy cream and 2 tablespoons honey; blend until smooth. Stir in 1½ teaspoons finely chopped mint leaves. Garnish well-chilled soup with strawberry slices and mint sprigs.
- To make mint sun-tea, fill a gallon glass jug with fresh water, then add 10 teabags and a couple handfuls of rinsed fresh mint sprigs. Brew in the sun for several hours before pouring over ice and garnishing with mint leaves.

Oregano

What is it?

Oregano, which is derived from the Greek phrase meaning "joy of the mountain," has long been associated with happiness. Originating in the Mediterranean, oregano is from the mint family, has many varieties, and is closely related to marjoram and thyme. The most common variety of oregano is also called "wild marjoram" and grows to 18 inches in height and spread. It is a hardy perennial with sprawling stems, clusters of tiny tubular pink or white flowers, and dark green, oval, paired, slightly hairy leaves. The leaves are harvested for their flavorful addition to Italian, Greek and Mexican dishes. Oregano was virtually unknown in the U.S. prior to WWII.

Flavor profile

Oregano is earthy and assertive with peppery hints of clove and balsam.

Growing & harvesting tips

+ Oregano is easy to grow from seeds, cuttings or division. Seeds require sunlight to germinate, so cover very lightly with soil.

+ Plant oregano in a sunny location with well-drained soil, which can be low in nutrients (not rich) and high in lime content.

+ Oregano is tolerant of most conditions. In the early months, make sure it does not dry out. After becoming established, plants handle dry conditions fairly well.

+ Oregano is well-suited to being grown in pots.

- Pinch back tops of plants to promote bushy growth.
- Pick oregano stems/leaves after the plant has reached at least 6 inches in height. For peak flavor, pick leaves just after flowers bud, but before they bloom.

Purchasing tips

Fresh oregano is readily available in most grocery stores. Look for bright bunches of oregano without blemishes or signs of wilting or yellowing. Dried oregano is quite flavorful and is an excellent substitute for fresh. Crumbled or ground oregano found in most spice aisles is generally a Mediterranean variety. It is sweeter, less pungent and not as strong as the Mexican variety which is available in Latin markets.

Storage & preservation tips

- Fresh oregano is highly perishable, so purchase only as needed. For short-term storage, immerse freshly cut stems in 2 inches of water, cover leaves loosely with plastic, and refrigerate for up to 3 days.
- Hang bunches of oregano by their stems or spread sprigs on a screen to dry in a warm, dark location. Store dried oregano in an airtight container in a cool, dark location for up to 6 months.
- Freeze oregano by one of two methods: wash and freeze sprigs, strip leaves from sprigs (discarding stems) and refreeze in bags; or chop leaves, mix with water and freeze in ice cube trays. Store the frozen cubes or leaves in freezer bags or airtight containers for up to 6 months.

Try it this way

- When using dried oregano, measure it first, then crush it in the palm of your hand, between your fingers or with a mortar and pestle to release the aromatic oils.
- Oregano retains more of its flavor if added closer to the completion of cooking.
- Make a Greek salad with greens, tomatoes, cucumbers, onions, feta cheese, and kalamata olives, sprinkled with fresh or dried oregano, oil and vinegar.
- Add finely chopped fresh oregano to your homemade burger or meatball mixtures, or sprinkle it on top of your favorite pizza.
- Sprinkle oregano on kabobs of lamb, pork, chicken or beef before grilling.

Parsley

What is it?

Parsley is a versatile and nutritious herb used in most of the world's cuisines. The best known of all garnishing herbs, it provides a beautiful appearance without distracting from the flavor of the food it adorns. Parsley is a biennial grown as an annual. Native to Central and Southern Europe, it grows from 12 to 18 inches tall and is generally one of two major types: English or Italian. English parsley is called curly parsley because of its dark green, ruffle-curled leaves. Italian parsley is called flat-leafed parsley due to its broad green leaf clusters.

Flavor profile

Parsley has a mild pepper flavor with a clean, refreshing taste.

Growing & harvesting tips

+ Purchase plants or start seeds in the spring. Seeds germinate slowly, so soak seeds with warm water for a few hours before planting. Use plug trays rather than seed trays, as parsley does not like transplanting.

+ Plant parsley in full sun and rich, deep, highly organic soil.

+ Parsley loves the outdoors and warm weather, but also loves moisture. Water well, especially during hot, dry periods.

+ Parsley is ideal for container growth, even in a kitchen window, if well-fed, watered and cut regularly.

+ Remove flower heads immediately to continue harvesting leaves.

- Harvest by clipping outer leaves from plants that are at least 8 inches tall, leaving the plant 2 to 3 inches in height. Cut regularly to encourage production.

Purchasing tips

Fresh and dried parsley are readily available. Fresh parsley should be bright green and crisp with no signs of wilting or yellowing. Dried parsley should have a deep green color and be free of stalks or yellow leaves.

Storage & preservation tips

- Fresh parsley can be stored in the refrigerator; however, the best storage method is simply to place stems in a glass of water on the counter. No refrigeration is required, and it makes an attractive kitchen display for up to 6 days. Change water daily.
- Successful home-drying of parsley is difficult. Store purchased dried parsley in an airtight container in a dry, dark location for up to 6 months.
- Frozen parsley maintains better flavor. Freeze by one of two methods: chop clean parsley, mix with water and freeze in ice cube trays; or freeze clean and pat-dried whole stalks. Store either product for up to 6 months in freezer bags or containers.

Try it this way

- Both leaves and the strong-flavored stems can be used in food preparation. Curly parsley is more often used as a garnish or chopped in sauces or salads, while flat-leaf is often used in cooking, due to its deep flavor and the ability to maintain that flavor when heated.
- A parsley garnish can be eaten as a palate cleanser.
- Stir chopped fresh parsley into buttered carrots or potatoes.
- Puree parsley with garlic, olive oil and ricotta cheese for use as a sauce on pasta, shellfish or cold beef.
- Combine chopped parsley with bulgar wheat, mint leaves, lemon juice and olive oil to make the well-known Middle Eastern dish, Tabbouleh.
- Use parsley as greenery in a fresh cut flower arrangement.

Rosemary

What is it?

Rosemary, meaning "dew of the sea," is steeped in myth, magic and folk medicine. Originating in the Mediterranean, it is widely cultivated in temperate regions for seasoning pork, lamb, soups, breads or biscuits. Its glossy, flat leaves resemble pine needles with a deep green color. Most varieties produce needles with a slightly silver underside and light blue flowers. This perennial shrub ranges from 1 to 6 feet tall, with some varieties growing prostrate and others growing upright. One interesting "lore" is that a rosemary plant will not live longer or grow taller than Jesus Christ.

Flavor profile

Rosemary has a peppery, warming and woody flavor with a sweet lemon-pine scent.

Growing & harvesting tips

+ Seeds can be difficult to germinate, so more success may be found with cuttings or by purchasing plants from a nursery.

+ If attempting to start by seed, plant in pots in a warm indoor location in the spring, taking care not to over-water. Leave potted through the first year, bringing indoors through the first winter.

+ Rosemary prefers fast drying soil and a sheltered, sunny, warm location.

+ Rosemary does well in containers, which is the preferred method of growth in cold climates. A prostrate and less hardy variety will look attractive and benefit from the extra protection of a container. Don't over-water it and fertilize it only after flowering. Move containers indoors during the winter and outdoors for the summer.

- Trim the tops occasionally to promote fuller growth. Remove frost-scorched portions of outdoor plants in the springtime. Never cut back in the fall.
- Harvest fresh leaves in moderation year-round. If large quantities of rosemary are needed, harvest in the summer for preservation.

Purchasing tips

Fresh rosemary is available year-round in large grocery stores. Look for pliable deep-green leaves, avoiding dry or brittle leaves and brown or yellow spots. Dried or ground rosemary is available in the spice aisle.

Storage & preservation tips

- Wrap fresh stems in damp paper towels, place in a plastic bag and refrigerate for up to 5 days; or place cut ends of sprigs in shallow water like a bouquet, gently wrap in plastic and refrigerate.
- To dry rosemary, spread sprigs on screens or hang to dry in a dark, warm location. Store sealed dried rosemary leaves in a dark, dry space for up to 6 months.
- Rosemary can be wrapped in foil and plastic and frozen for up to 3 months.

Try it this way

- Finely chop the leaves to season dishes or use the entire woody stems (with leaves) to flavor soups and stews. Remove stems or sharp whole dried leaves (by straining) before serving; or finely chop dried leaves before use.
- Use stripped rosemary sprigs as flavorful skewers for grilled shrimp, scallops, lamb or chicken.
- Roast potatoes in the oven with olive oil, rosemary and garlic.
- Add a fresh sprig to boiling water when cooking rice.
- To make a refreshing punch, heat 2 cups of water with 2 handfuls of fresh rosemary sprigs to boiling. Simmer 5 minutes, then cool and strain. Add 12 ounces frozen pineapple juice to the liquid and chill. Add 1 liter of ginger ale just before serving.
- Puree fresh rosemary leaves and add to olive oil for bread dipping.

Sage

What is it?

Sage, specifically the variety known as garden sage or common sage, is a perennial evergreen shrub with woody stems, pairs of fuzzy oval gray-green leaves, spiky mauve and blue flowers and a height of 2 feet. This variety is the best-known for its culinary use in stuffing or seasoning poultry, pork, lamb, cheeses, drinks or soups. There are numerous varieties of sage grown around the world with many different sizes, colors and growing preferences.

Flavor profile

Sage is pungent with a slightly peppery flavor. It is sometimes known for being bitter, with a musty mint taste and aroma.

Growing & harvesting tips

+ Start the common sage variety with seed indoors up to eight weeks before the last frost, or sow seeds outdoors after the threat of frost has passed. Always use fresh seeds. Propagation by cuttings also works well for many varieties of sage.

+ Young plants require steady moisture until mature, then thrive in well-drained soil. Sage is drought-tolerant once established and enjoys sun.

+ Sage will withstand winters best if planted in well-drained, non-acidic soil in a warm, dry and protected area.

+ Sages work well for container gardening. Fertilize only after flowering and do not over-water.

- Prune in late spring or after flowering in late summer, but never in the fall.
- Sage degenerates over time, becoming thick and woody; replace sage plants every 3 to 4 years.
- Since it is an evergreen, sage can be harvested throughout the year. Cut sage just above the new growth line. Don't cut old, woody growth for cooking.

Purchasing tips

Small bunches of fresh sage are available year-round in many grocery stores. Choose leaves that are aromatic with no soft spots, wilting or dried edges. Dried sage is available whole, rubbed (crumbled) and ground. Rubbed sage has a light, velvety appearance. Fresh leaves taste lighter and less musty than dried sage.

Storage & preservation tips

- Wrap fresh sage leaves in a paper towel and seal in a plastic bag to refrigerate for up to 4 days.
- To dry sage, hang stalks in a dark, well-ventilated area until the leaves crumble easily; then store in tightly sealed containers in a cool, dark location for up to 6 months. Dried sage can pick up a musty scent and flavor, so test it before use and discard if inferior.
- Sage can be frozen for up to 6 months; freeze leaves or stalks individually on a tray before placing in a sealed freezer bag or container.

Try it this way

- To provide flavor to poultry, place fresh or dried sage leaves under the skin or in the roasting dishes.
- Add thinly sliced sage to potato, mixed greens or pasta salads for an interesting and flavorful twist.
- For a yummy omelet, add 1 teaspoon chopped fresh sage, 2 tablespoons water, ¼ cup cubed ham, and salt and pepper to 3 beaten eggs. After cooking the mixture in a hot buttered skillet just until the surface is almost set, fold the omelet in half over 2 to 3 slices brie cheese and cook until cheese is melted.
- Fry sage leaves for a snack or garnish. Heat ½ cup vegetable oil over medium heat and lightly dust sage leaves with flour, shaking off excess. Drop leaves into hot oil and cook until crispy and bright green, about 30 seconds; remove and drain on paper towels.

Savory

What is it?

There are two main culinary varieties of savory – summer savory and winter savory. Summer savory is an annual with petite gray-green leaves and small white-pink flowers. Winter savory is a woodier, bitter perennial with small, compact, bright green foliage and tiny spikes of white flowers. Savory is a Mediterranean native, reaching no more than two feet in height. Known as the "bean herb," it frequently adds richness to legume, meat, and vegetable dishes, such as stews or soups.

Flavor profile

Savory is aromatic with peppery and minty qualities. Summer savory is lighter, smoother and more commonly used in cooking, while winter savory is stronger, bitterer and a bit piney.

Growing & harvesting tips

+ Savory enjoys full sun and well-drained soil. Summer savory prefers more water and nutrient-rich soil, while winter savory can handle less water and nutrient-poor soil.

+ Summer and winter savory can be sown by seed. Cuttings can also be used to propagate the winter variety. Seeds should not be covered by soil, since they require sunlight to germinate.

+ Do not feed savory liquid fertilizer, as it will likely cause the plant to fail.

+ Savories work well for container gardening.

- Winter savory makes a good edging plant and can be harvested anytime.
- Begin harvesting summer savory for immediate use after it reaches at least 6 inches tall. Just before the flowers bud, harvest the top 6 to 8 inches for drying. Pruning and harvesting maintains flavor and encourages fullness.

Purchasing tips

Fresh savory can be purchased in specialty markets and some large grocery stores. Summer savory is best used fresh. Choose savory that smells sharp, clean and fresh, without signs of brown spots or wilting. Savory can also be purchased dried or crushed in the spice aisle.

Storage & preservation tips

- Wrap fresh savory in damp paper towels inside a loosely closed plastic bag to refrigerate for up to 1 week.
- Summer savory dries easily. Spread sprigs on screens or hang stems upside down in a warm, dry, dark location. Store dried savory in an airtight container in a cool, dry location for up to 6 months.
- To freeze, puree clean savory leaves with olive oil or butter and freeze in ice cube trays. Pop out frozen cubes to store in a sealed freezer bag for up to 2 months.

Try it this way

- Summer savory should be added near the end of cooking, while winter savory should stew longer.
- Summer savory can replace both salt and pepper when preparing cooked dishes, which can be helpful for those on a salt-free diet.
- Add a sprig of savory to water when cooking green, wax or lima beans.
- Mix chopped savory with grated lemon and add it to bread crumbs for a great fish coating.
- Make a summer salad with steamed green beans, cherry tomatoes, kalamata olives, garlic and a sprig of chopped summer savory tossed with olive oil.

Sorrel

What is it?

Sorrel is a slightly lemon-flavored green herb, sometimes grown as a vegetable. Its leaves are commonly used in salads or for flavoring soup. While varieties of sorrel differ, garden sorrel, also called common sorrel, is a fairly coarse-looking hardy perennial with 6-inch sword-shaped leaves and a plant height of 2 feet. It is a native of Europe, Asia and North America that has been naturalized in many countries throughout the world.

Flavor profile

Sorrel is sharp and somewhat bitter with a tart citrus tang.

Growing & harvesting tips

+ Grow sorrel in full sun to partial shade with deep, rich, moist, well-drained and acid soil.
+ Propagate seeds under protection in the early spring. Transplant when plants are large enough to handle and soil has warmed. Sorrel can also be started by root division.
+ Divide plants every 2 to 3 years for renewal, and replace plants every 4 to 5 years, due to the tendency to become woody.
+ Cull unwanted plants and remove flowers to prevent self-seeding and to keep leaves succulent. Plant sorrel in contained areas to prevent them from becoming like weeds.
+ When hot, sorrel becomes bitter, so keep soil moist and cool with regular watering and mulch.
+ Harvest young leaves throughout the growing season.

Purchasing tips

Fresh sorrel is sometimes available in large grocery stores or specialty markets. Look for firm, bright green, crisp leaves that are free from woody-looking stems or yellow or wilted leaves. Sorrel is not available in a dried form. Occasionally, gourmet stores carry cooked sorrel in jars or cans.

Storage & preservation tips

+ Fresh sorrel can be refrigerated in a paper-towel-lined plastic bag for up to 3 days.
+ Freeze by one of two methods: puree clean sorrel with a small amount of water, spoon into ice cube trays, and pop out frozen cubes; or freeze clean, pat-dried and paper towel wrapped sorrel leaves. Store either product for up to 6 months in sealed freezer bags or containers.

Try it this way

+ Because of its strong flavor, add sorrel to your dishes sparingly, tasting as you go.
+ Enhance the flavor of lamb, veal, pork, duck, goose, fish and shell fish by seasoning with sorrel.
+ Add fresh young leaves to a sandwich, combine sorrel with other herbs in salads, or make the French culinary classic, Sorrel Soup.
+ Substitute sorrel for spinach in a favorite omelet, soufflé or sauce recipe.
+ Tenderize meat with sorrel by wrapping it around steak or adding crushed fresh leaves to a marinade.

Special notes

+ Consume sorrel in moderation. Very large doses are poisonous, causing severe kidney damage. It may also not be good for those with rheumatism, arthritis, gout, kidney stones or gastric hyperacidity. Its leaves may also cause contact dermatitis.
+ Due to its high acid level, sorrel can cause a reaction in some metals, such as discoloration of carbon steel knifes, aluminum, iron and silver. Avoid using aluminum or cast iron cookware.

Tarragon

What is it?

Tarragon's flavorful leaves are an essential ingredient in French cuisine. Native to Southern Europe, French tarragon is the most widely-used culinary variety. Like other varieties of tarragon, it has long, narrow green leaves. Mexican (winter) tarragon is indigenous to Mexico and is the "marigold of the herb garden" because of its bright gold summer flowers. Tarragon grows 2 to 4 feet tall, with most varieties being tender or half-hardy perennials, requiring extra care during the winter. While French and Mexican tarragons can be used fairly interchangeably, Russian tarragon is considered inferior for culinary purposes.

Flavor profile

Tarragon has the sweet, delicate licorice flavor of anise; French is considered to have superior flavor, while Mexican is a bit spicier with an accent of cinnamon.

Growing & harvesting tips

+ French tarragon does not produce viable seed; it must be propagated from cuttings or can sometimes be established by division. Mexican tarragon can be started with seed or cuttings. Start seedlings indoors in a controlled environment and plant outdoors after the temperature will not fall below 50°F at night.

+ When purchasing plants, beware of rust and purchase the largest seedlings available.

+ Tarragon prefers full sun, well-drained soil and a warm, dry climate.

- Because of their climate sensitivity, both varieties work well for container gardening. Mexican tarragon likes to be root-bound, while French tarragon does not, so plan pot sizes accordingly. Move container tarragon to a cool frost-free environment for cold winters or provide frost cloth, mulch, or straw for tarragon through warm winters. Do not water during its dormant season.
- Divide tarragon every few years for the best growth.
- To harvest, pick leaves throughout the growing season for fresh use and during mid-season for preservation.

Purchasing tips

Fresh, dried and ground tarragon are available year-round in most grocery stores or specialty markets. Fresh tarragon should be green without sign of brown spots or wilting.

Storage & preservation tips

- To refrigerate fresh tarragon, wrap leaves loosely in a barely damp paper towel and place in a sealed plastic bag filled with air, or stand fresh stems in shallow water and cover loosely with plastic for up to 5 days.
- Mexican tarragon dries well, while French does not. Hang stems of tarragon upside down to dry. Store in an airtight container for up to 6 months in a cool, dark location.
- Tarragon can be frozen by placing clean and pat-dried leaves in freezer bags or by chopping them finely and adding to shallow water in an ice cube tray. Pop out frozen cubes to store in freezer bags for up to 3 months.

Try it this way

- Add tarragon sparingly, near the end of cooking.
- Tarragon complements mushrooms, asparagus, eggs, poultry and shellfish and is an ingredient in the classic French béarnaise sauce.
- Mix finely chopped tarragon with butter, chives and lemon juice for a fish or chicken marinade.
- Scramble eggs with tomatoes, mozzarella and fresh tarragon.
- The flowers of Mexican tarragon can be added to green salads.
- Add chopped fresh tarragon to chicken salad, mashed potatoes or deviled eggs for new excitement in an old classic.

Thyme

What is it?

Thyme is a hardy evergreen perennial, native to the Mediterranean, but widely grown elsewhere. Numerous varieties are available with subtle differences in taste, purpose and appearance. French thyme, or garden thyme, is most commonly used for culinary purposes. Typically growing up to 12 inches in height, thyme has white to purple flowers and gray-green, dark-green or silver petite leaves, which can be narrow or wide. The flavorful leaves are used to season stuffing, sauce, soup, meat and fish.

Flavor profile

Thyme is slightly minty with a sometimes pungent clove-like taste. Other subtle flavors are sometimes present in different varieties, such as lemon thyme or caraway thyme.

Growing & harvesting tips

+ Germination by seed can be slow and uneven, therefore it is best to make cuttings from new growth in the spring, divide creeping varieties, or purchase new seedlings.

+ Use sandy, well-drained, low-nutrient soil when growing thyme, as it is a drought-loving plant requiring minimal watering. Plant in full sun.

+ Cut back foliage by a third in the spring and continue with light trimmings throughout the growing season to promote lush growth.

+ Although thyme is a perennial, a cold or wet winter climate can be difficult; protect plants by keeping them dry and warm with mulch, or move container-grown thyme indoors.

Water only sparingly through the winter. All varieties of thyme are suited to container gardening.

+ Harvest thyme throughout the growing season, snipping sprigs as needed. Leaves are sweetest just before flowers appear. Stripping fresh leaves can be tedious, so dry the stems just until brittle and then gently rub between palms to remove leaves.

Purchasing tips

Fresh, dried and ground thyme can be purchased year-round in most grocery stores. When selecting fresh thyme, choose sprigs with strong green color and avoid any signs of wilting, dark spots or yellowing. Whenever possible, purchase fresh rather than dry.

Storage & preservation tips

+ Fresh thyme should be placed inside a plastic bag with a barely damp paper towel and stored in the refrigerator for up to 5 days.

+ To dry, hang bundles of thyme sprigs upside down or spread on screens in a warm, dry and airy location for about 10 days. Store dried leaves in a tightly sealed container for up to 6 months.

+ Thyme can be frozen by placing cleaned, pat-dried and paper towel wrapped leaves in freezer bags or by chopping finely and adding to shallow water in an ice cube tray. Pop out frozen cubes to store in freezer bags for up to 3 months.

Try it this way

+ Thyme is a wonderful complementary herb, so combine it with rosemary or sage for a more complex flavor.

+ Add thyme early in the cooking process so its oils have time to be released. For example, slice zucchini lengthwise, drizzle with olive oil and sprinkle with salt, pepper and chopped fresh thyme leaves before roasting.

+ Drizzle watermelon cubes with Balsamic syrup, then sprinkle with lemon thyme, a little sea salt and cracked black pepper for a summer salad.

+ Make yummy herb biscuits by adding a small amount of dried thyme and sage to your favorite recipe.

CLASSIC HERB COMBINATIONS

Fines herbs: chives, tarragon, chervil and parsley, chopped and mixed together in equal parts

Herbes de Provence: many variations of this dried herb blend exist, but one suggested blend includes thyme, sage, rosemary, lavender and fennel seeds

Bouquet garni: fresh herbs usually including bay leaf, thyme and parsley, tied in a bundle or placed in a piece of cheesecloth and used to season sauce or stock and removed before serving

TERMS

+ **Perennial** plants live for many growing seasons, coming back yearly; **biennial** plants generally produce only foliage the first year, and then bloom, bear fruit and die off the second year; and **annuals** complete their life cycle in one growing season.

+ **Zones** are used to communicate regional climate information. Know your specific zone and use that information as you purchase plants and seeds.

+ **Transplanting** is the process of removing and resetting a plant, sometimes from a garden or sometimes from a pot or seed tray.

+ **Successive planting** is a method for having a continuous supply of a particular herb. By starting batches of seeds at different times, the plants will mature at different times as well. This is often suggested if the plant requires a short time to mature or grows in climates with long growing seasons.

+ **Plug trays** have individualized compartments for each seedling, while **seed trays** are open with one shared space for all the seedlings. When seedlings have an aversion to transplanting, either due to a long tap root or roots that don't like to be separated/handled, plug trays are more successful.

+ **Propagation** is simply plant reproduction accomplished through seeds, cuttings, division or layering. **Cuttings** are pieces of a mature plant, severed with a sharp blade or knife, allowed to generate growth to establish a new plant. Stem cuttings can be taken anytime from soft tissue plants (see mint p. 42). Hard tissue cuttings are made from spring through fall, dependent on the plant variety. Root cuttings can be made in the spring and fall. **Division,** by digging mature plants and separating the roots, can produce two or more new plants. **Layering** works well for plants with flexible stems, such as bay, rosemary and sage. This process calls for burying the tip of the stem of an existing plant while still connected to the original plant. After the buried tip forms new roots, it can be detached for replanting.